DON BRECKON'S
GREAT WESTERN RAILWAY

Leyland 'Lion' & Collett 060

DON BRECKON'S GREAT WESTERN RAILWAY

DAVID & CHARLES

Newton Abbot   London   North Pomfret (Vt)

To Ian, David and Christopher

Jacket photograph of author by Paul Broadhurst

British Library Cataloguing in Publication Data

Breckon, Don
    Don Breckon's Great Western Railway.
    1. Great Western Railway—Pictorial works
    I. Title
    385′.0942   HE3020.G8
    ISBN 0-7153-8872-X

Typeset by P&M Typesetting Ltd Exeter Devon
and printed in The Netherlands
by Royal Smeets Offset Weert
for David & Charles Publishers plc
Brunel House Newton Abbot Devon

Published in the United States of America
by David & Charles Inc
North Pomfret Vermont 05053 USA

CONTENTS

THE PAINTINGS

ACKNOWLEDGEMENTS

Thanks are due to the following, who have lent paintings for reproduction in the book:

David & Anne-Marie Rouse	'Day Trip'
Mr Richard Gee	'Waiting at Dymock'
	'Crossing the Cornfield'
	'Country Pannier'
Mr L. Rollason	'Waiting at Witney'
Mr & Mrs M. R. Jacobs	'Double Header at Dainton'
Mr & Mrs C. F. Seaton	'Passing the Farm'
Mr & Mrs J. L. Ellis	'Somerset Freight'
Frank & Sonia Eden	'Picnic'
Peter & Beryl Downe	'Vale of Rheidol'
	'Swindon Roundhouse'
Mr David St John Thomas	'The Train and the Sea'
	'Dulverton Station'
	'Royal Train Crossing Barmouth Bridge'
Burnley & Eileen Moses	'Meeting the Train'
Bernice & Brian Long	'Driver's View'
Bishop's Waltham Gallery	'Evening Service'
Mr Jim Harries	*Dumbleton Hall* leaving Kingswear'
Mr & Mrs G. H. Batchelor	'Engines at Swindon'
4160 Ltd (Preservation Soc.)	'Coasting Home'
Carol & Ian Kitt	'Passing St Winnow'
Mr & Mrs B. W. Dawson	'Country Connection'

'Changing Trains', 'Broad Gauge at Paddington' and 'Night Train' are in private collections.

Acknowledgement is also due to:

Solomon and Whitehead (Guild Prints) Ltd, who have allowed us to reproduce the original paintings 'Changing Trains', 'Broad Gauge at Paddington', and 'Country Connection'. These pictures are available in print form. Also *Dumbleton Hall* leaving Kingswear' which is produced as a limited edition print published by Solomon and Whitehead (Guild Prints) Ltd who own the copyrights.

4160 Ltd who have allowed us to reproduce the original painting 'Coasting Home' which is available as a limited edition print.

PUBLISHER'S PREFACE

When I was a boy, the route into town varied according to whether it was warm enough for the owners of a terraced house to have their front door open. Many people made a point of peeping into the outer hall, where a colourful painting of a Great Western Railway express hung opposite the coat hooks. Feelings were curious. A few hundred yards further down the hill one could see the real thing: green locomotives with sexy tapering boilers and shining copper domes, pulling rakes of inevitably-varied chocolate-and-cream coaches. Yet the fact that you enjoyed the real thing made you believe you should make the best of the painting too; and how I coveted it. Not merely for the present but as a record for the days when things changed; for before the war there had been a plan to electrify everything in the South West, and now there were the first rumblings about nationalisation and dieselisation. How I coveted it, and yet how I despised it! Even if it had been invented then the phrase 'chocolate-box art' was certainly not yet known to me, but it sums up my criticism. The painting was only a glorified photograph and not a very accurate one at that. The shades of chocolate-and-cream were positively wrong, the chocolate almost black, the cream so anaemic, and the engine looked as though it might fall between the rails. The final feeling was that some day someone *must* properly portray the Great Western as Constable did his countryside.

Now, I am not going to call Don Breckon the Constable of the Great Western. Anyway, he is more of the Turner school! But he is undoubtedly *the* artist of God's Wonderful Railway, and few books have given me such pleasure to bring to publication as this. What has been particularly rewarding has been working with Don and understanding what it is that makes him such an unusual man—and then being part of his grand plan to enhance the Great Western's visual image.

As I said in my Preface to his first book, *The Railway Paintings of Don Breckon*, published four years ago and now out of print, we are dealing with a technical perfectionist who yet is a real artist. He spares no pains to get the nuts and bolts right; you almost have to be an engineer to keep up with him. But while some of his paintings may be of places he has never visited, so that he relies on photographs and technical data, they catch the very soul of the Great Western in its varied moods. Thus the painting he undertook for me of a busy scene at Dulverton on the Taunton-Barnstaple branch is (as he says in his commentary) based on photographic evidence; yet there is no way it could possibly have been painted by someone who did not love, respect and intimately know and understand the GWR. The subject and the artist seem to become almost inseparable. Every detail is worthy of close inspection. You hear the sounds and smell the steam and smoke, you relive some of the GWR's idiosyncrasies, and realise how important was the train in the life of the countryside as well as town. Even the staff are clearly Great Western, not just any railwaymen, proud of the task handed down by Brunel and Gooch.

That there is depth in Don Breckon's work has been obvious to me since a decade-and-a-half ago a colleague told me I should urgently visit a gallery where one of his early paintings was hanging. Every time I have gone up or down my stairs since, it has given me fresh pleasure; again, it lives. It too, a sea-splashed express between Dawlish and Teignmouth, is included in this collection.

Here you see the Great Western in many moods. Of course you will buy the book for the paintings, but an added bonus is that while Don did not think he could write an introductory text for his first book, here he has enthusiastically done so. He wrote it to time, moreover. He may be a perfectionist, and he knows what he wants. That, incidentally, is distinctly not the glare of publicity: I hope to get this past him in the morning, when he returns my paintings after their visit to the colour process house. But, no doubt helped by his wife Meg, he is also very professional in his Lostwithiel studio. He is seldom a day late, which is the publisher's final accolade.

David St John Thomas
Brunel House
Newton Abbot

INTRODUCTION

Train Spotters

Train Spotting

Train spotting was rather like bird watching or fishing. We would travel miles for a rare catch but would then have to wait patiently for long periods when nothing seemed to be happening. Even today groups of boys can be seen at the end of some station platforms, but they are a mere platoon in comparison to the regiments of train spotters in the days of steam. At that time most stations on main lines had their complement of schoolboys lurking around corners or boldly monopolising luggage trolleys along the platform. Now most of the train spotters and many of the stations have gone and today's trains flash past unheeded.

I was born and brought up in Northamptonshire and my train spotting days in the late 1940s were mainly on the old Midland line from St Pancras to the north. The interest in 'watching the trains go by' combined with boys' natural instinct for collecting turned us rapidly into enthusiasts. Unlike my friends, however, I was never very interested in writing engine numbers down in my note-book. I was looking for an engine with a *name*. Once a locomotive acquired a nameplate it took on a personality and an instant air of importance. Perhaps the names didn't always seem to have much connection with a steam locomotive and perhaps we seldom had any idea what, or where, or who, the name commemorated—it was still a name. Passengers must have been bemused to hear train spotters excitedly shouting 'Gilbert and Ellice Islands' or trying to pronounce 'Tyrwhitt' on Kettering station!

Great Western nameplates were the finest of all with bold letters set off with brass beading. Some railways seemed to fasten the name on as an afterthought but the Great Western gave the

9

impression that they started with the nameplate and built the engine around it.

Looking back now on those days of train spotting I realise that there was a strong moral aspect of the hobby that never really struck me at the time. There was no referee to check the little book of numbers, and yet while neatly underlining the names of the day's sightings and looking longingly for all those engines not yet seen it never occurred to us to cheat by adding a few extra! Just to do it once would have cancelled out the whole exercise. It didn't mean though that we didn't suspect one another at times. The story of *Llanthony Abbey* is a case in point.

My brother-in-law was brought up in Bristol and as a youth was a very keen train spotter. He and his cousin used to haunt Bristol Temple Meads which must have been one of the best locations on the Great Western for seeing trains. They were so keen that eventually they had every single Castle class engine marked down in their books except one. *Llanthony Abbey* was a Stafford Road engine and had never showed its smoke-box in Bristol when Peter and Geoff were around to see it. Then came the day when Peter went to Temple Meads by himself and from the end of the platform scanned the engines in the shed. He couldn't believe it when he saw 5088 on the buffer beam, but quite soon the engine steamed slowly out of the shed yard and it was indeed the elusive *Llanthony Abbey*—his list was complete. He couldn't wait to tell Geoff who promptly refused to believe him. In fact they weren't on speaking terms for some time. Even in youth the British take their pleasures very seriously!

On the Midland line in those days the named engines were the Jubilee class and they were the ones I was looking for. The Black Fives were more numerous and I must admit looked more powerful than the Jubilees but they didn't have names. We called them 'Blackie Tapers' because of their tapered boilers. After school we played football or cricket on a piece of waste ground and only welcomed two interruptions to our game. One was the evening episode of *Dick Barton* on the radio and the other was the northbound express which came through Corby in the early evening. We would sprint down to the railway bridge and sit on a pile of sleepers beside the line staring expectantly down the long straight for the first sign of smoke against

the distant overbridge. At last it could be seen and steadily it grew larger. Guesses came thick and fast. 'It's a Blackie', 'No it's a Jube', 'It is'. As the train rushed past five pairs of eyes zoomed in on the curved nameplate over the leading driving wheel. *Galatea* or *Bellerophon* was chorused and then often followed by a dejected 'I've got it' or the exultant first sighting cry of 'A Cop ...' This was followed by the quiet satisfaction of going home and taking fountain pen and ruler to underline neatly the name and number of the engine in the *ABC of British Railways, London Midland and Scottish Regions* book, (price 2s). We all had these little books and it was because of a particular photograph in it that we were to be seen one evening dancing in the road like a tribe of dervishes.

There were several photographs of locomotives among the lists of engine names and numbers, and one was a dramatic shot of a Patriot class No 45538—*Giggleswick*. Though hardly the most inspiring of locomotive names we stared at that picture with the enthusiasm that would be reserved later for the film poster of Jane Russell in *The Outlaw*. It had smoke deflectors which we called wind-shields or even 'blinkers', a sure sign, we thought, of a really powerful engine. We had never

seen a Patriot on our line but there were rumours that they made the occasional appearance.

One evening we were late getting away from our football game and had to rush down to the bridge to see the express coming along the embankment. 'Blinkers', someone cried and we thundered on like the Seventh Cavalry as we saw that it was indeed a 'Patriot'. We pulled up gasping as the train roared over the bridge above us. We were too far off to read the nameplate but we knew that number on the cabside by heart—45538. There followed a delirious war dance which caused passing motorists some concern. They were not to know that it was only a bunch of train spotters celebrating a prize Cop!

Train spotters everywhere had favourite spots which for periods of time became guarded locations for each group until the novelty wore off and a new place was sought. We made many trips to a shallow cutting where the Leicester and Nottingham lines divided about six miles south-west of Corby. This was our favourite place for those long summer days of train spotting. Arriving on our bikes along the gated road which ran parallel with the line we unloaded our supplies of food and drink and slipped over the fence. If there was no unfriendly shout from the signal box we edged down slowly to our

Lineside Workers

target area which was halfway down the embankment. Settled in among the long grass we arranged our packets of sandwiches, bottles of 'Tizer' or ginger beer, and our note-books around us and waited for the first event.

The ting of bells from the signal box and the creak of signal wires brought the heads up. The approaching train was identified as 'only a freight', 'passenger', or if there was a sound of power and speed, 'express'. Endless trains of coal wagons brought only a passing interest. We just wanted them out of the way to clear the road for trains headed by engines with nameplates. In between the activity on the line we lay in the grass munching and swapping sandwiches, discussing trains and trying to remember the words of 'Ghost riders in the sky'. Occasionally scuffles would break out but these were limited by the fear of a shouted 'Clear off' from the signal box. In those days an angry shout from an adult would send small boys scampering off over the horizon.

So the long afternoons went by until we felt that it must be teatime and we cycled off home, always hating that last express which was to be heard roaring through just as we were out of sight of the line. Time spent train spotting leaves its mark on the memory, and tucked away in many homes

11

there are probably dog-eared books of locomotives with many of the names and numbers neatly underlined.

Painting Trains

When my father was home on leave from the army during the war he taught me how to draw ships. He drew two lines tapering towards a point and then fitted the outline of a ship between these lines. Starting with the bow, where the lines were widest apart, and drawing superstructure and funnels his detail became smaller and smaller down towards the point. I was amazed. The ship was sailing out of the paper and it seemed to be five miles long! I copied Dad's drawing over and over again fascinated by the feeling of distance and the discovery of a three-dimensional effect. Without knowing it I had been introduced to perspective, and with a few modifications drawings of long ships could become drawings of long trains with coaches running back to a distant horizon.

For boys growing up in the 1940s there seemed to be definite areas of interest which absorbed us all totally until some new passion came along. The difference then was that the shops were unable to stock their shelves with bright new toys even if there had been money to buy them. So we played football in the street with an old tennis ball if we were lucky, and an old tin can if we weren't. Games of cowboys and Indians—inspired by the Saturday morning pictures—saw us all with bits of stick roughly shaped to resemble the gun and treasured for weeks as if they were the real thing. On our way home from school we would lean over the bridge as the engines from the steelworks blasted underneath, delighting us with the clouds of dense smoke sent to engulf us. The steelworks dominated the town of Corby where I lived and at that time the industrial tank engines heaved molten metal and red hot slag in and out of the works in special container wagons. We watched the metal slop and splash, smelled the smoke from the train and dreamed of far off places and holidays.

So our games were fuelled by imagination and for me this helped to sharpen my one constant interest—drawing. The world of make-believe in our games carried over into paper and pencil to the extent that my drawings were often accompanied by

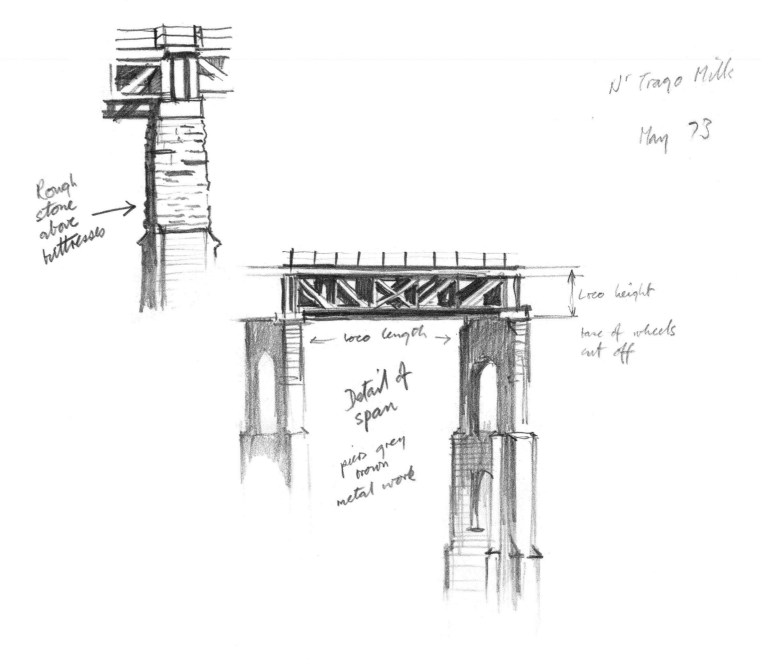

appropriate sound effects to the amusement or irritation of my parents. In the days before television the best place for a small boy was sprawled on the rug in front of the fire with *Every Boy's Wonder Book* of something-or-other and a drawing book and pencils. There seemed a lot of 'wonder' about then and the pages of my drawing books were filled with great air battles mingled with trains, and the evenings seemed to last forever.

As we grew older trips to the lineside in the train-spotting days increased the interest in drawing trains, very often all at the wrong time. They began to appear in the margins of my school books. Drawing can be so absorbing even when the results are simple small sketches in the corner of the page. I remember a day when I was engrossed in a little 'doodle' during a Latin lesson. A gradual silence had settled over the room as the master became

Breakers' Yard.

of artwork and no jobs forthcoming. Security in a job, plus respectability, was the aim in those days so when the school nudged me in the direction of an art teachers' training college it seemed the best road to follow. It also left the commercial art option open by giving me what I thought would be a general art training.

Drawing and painting now became more serious as examinations approached though my 'A' level art work was carried out in the school boiler room due to lack of accommodation. We did precious little work in between reading *Cycling* magazine and chatting with the caretaker! Nevertheless I must have done enough to be called for an interview at the Bath Academy of Art.

I travelled on a Great Western train for the first time for this interview day in Bath. I had seen Paddington for the first time too. Ever since then whenever I found myself in London with spare time I would be drawn there to enjoy that particular atmosphere. I saw Castles and Kings at the buffer stops, and waiting at the other end of the station, heading westbound, expresses. How lucky it was that I had chosen Bath and that they offered me a place. My association with the Great Western Railway began on that day in 1954 and has continued ever since. For the moment, however, having secured my future at college, I had then to go off for two years' national service in the RAF at Patrington in Yorkshire. Further glimpses of the Great Western would have to wait.

During the following years of national service, followed by art training, and finally the start of my teaching career in Bedford I had become used to the railway as a means of travel. Other interests had once again taken over and new passions discovered. I had been introduced to totally new concepts in art, and my painting which had been so photographic in style had changed completely.

Collecting photographs of cities by night for reference material I was excited by the weaving patterns of the lights of cars which appeared in time-exposure shots of night streets and roundabouts. They gave a feeling of movement and space but they also had echoes of interweaving railway tracks at junctions. This suited my style at the time and I painted 'Terminus' which was an impression of the approach to a station at night with signal lights reflecting off the rails. I entered it in a painting competition in

aware that one member of his class was not with him. It took me a little time to realise that not only had the lesson stopped but that I had become the focus of attention. The Latin master peered at the drawing, sighed, and went on with the lesson. I expect he was resigned to the fact that I was no great loss to Latin.

As my interest in trains began to compete with a new passion for cycling, and the margins began to fill with Tour de France racers it was at this time that I began to think about a future career in art. I was quite good at cartoons and posters and my first thought was that I would like to be a commercial artist. This seemed to be the title given to anyone who was an artist but didn't actually sell paintings for a living. A relative put me off this idea somewhat by the lurid description of a friend of hers who had wandered around London for years with a portfolio

Kettering and was delighted when it won the 'Salisbury Prize' for that year. This was a gentle nudge towards the idea that railways could become the subject of future paintings.

The abstract approach also adapted to a new and melancholy aspect—the breaker's yard. I visited Cohens at Kettering and Barry in South Wales, and among the depressing sights of partly dismantled locomotives found the shapes of sliced wheels and connecting rods were instant compositions of railway flavoured abstraction. I found that pure abstract painting could be dramatic but in the end it was unsatisfactory for me. The need for the shapes and forms to relate to the images of life was strong and it was difficult to come to terms with the dictum

that 'art must go forward' when my interests lay more and more with the scenes from the past! The use of photographs, frowned on in the 1950s, became accepted in the work of artists of the 1960s, even to the extent of sticking cut-outs from magazines directly onto the canvas. I embarked on several of these photo-montage 'paintings' and it wasn't long before railways were creeping into the compositions. Painting is perhaps a loose description of what was going on because aerosol cans, stencils, printing and gluing were all involved!

As steam declined my interest increased, and I travelled on several specials on the southern and western regions. From scrapyards to preserved lines and from disused stations to Shap summit, I was

becoming more and more immersed in the aspect of railways which was fast disappearing. I wanted to work this interest into my paintings and the abstract approach was no longer satisfying. Any lingering doubts about the straightforward representation of steam locomotives in paintings started to fade when I saw an exhibition of Terence Cuneo's work at the Clapham Museum of Transport. Here was life, character and self-expression without resort to abstraction. I didn't realise it at the time but the course of my work and my life was changing. Not long afterwards I gave a friend of mine, as a wedding present, a photo-montage of bits of trains forming a design of wheels and connecting rods. As he wasn't a railway enthusiast he accepted it remarkably calmly. 'If you like trains so much why don't you just paint them,' he said. 'Ah well...' I replied, but couldn't think of a reason. For some time as I drove back and forward to school in Reading where I was teaching his words came back to me and I continued to wonder.

Another nudge towards a change of direction came from a television programme. The BBC screened *The Man Who Loved Giants*, a programme about the life and work of David Shepherd. I was very impressed. At school the next day the subject of the programme came up in the staff room. 'See that chap David Shepherd,' said the science teacher dolefully, 'what a life—eh? It's all right for him.' Yes—I thought—it would be all right for me too!

I think that it is a combination of small things rather than one big event which affects the course of our lives. It was just such a collection which caused me to give up my job, sell the house and set off with Meg and our first son Ian on a camping tour of England and Scotland which would lead to we knew not where! It was rather like shuffling the cards in life to see what new hand we came up with. It was an exciting thing to do and we have never regretted it. It was at this time, with all the conventional restraints and influences gone, that the final steps towards what was to become my future career were finally made.

During our travels I had worked on a straightforward portrait of a steam locomotive. We had stopped in Bristol to see my father-in-law and the painting was propped on the easel in the back garden to dry. The man who lived next door asked if he could buy it and I took this to be a good omen.

Thus encouraged I set out to the local galleries with a selection of work amongst which were railway paintings. But the gallery owners were sceptical. 'Railways! There's no demand for these. You have to be very careful about detail, you know, these enthusiasts are fanatics!' Rather to everyone's surprise the paintings proved so popular that I was soon being asked to paint only railway subjects. To be earning a living as an artist was a wonderful feeling, but to be doing so by painting steam trains was unbelievable.

Since that time I have gone on exploring not just railways of the past but increasingly what goes on around the railway. I have pulled back from the trains to see more of the landscape, and the people going about their activities of work and play. The train remains the focal point but I hope that it now relates more to its surroundings so that the scene can be visualised before the train has appeared, when it is only a sound in the distance, and after it has passed with just the smoke clinging around the trees. In this way there can be a feeling of a moment in time, the landscape glimpsed from the train and the train glimpsed from the landscape. An interesting aspect of the development of the setting is that the atmosphere of the period can be recalled by working in farm machinery, or cars, or small but significant things which bring the exclamation—'I remember those days'.

After we finally settled in Cornwall the landscape of the Westcountry and its relationship to the railway made a slow but steady impression on my work. The wooded hills rose steeply from the line, the track curved continually crossing deep little valleys on high masonry viaducts. Even the diesel locomotives sounded as though it was hard work. The rolling open landscape of Northamptonshire, which I had known so well from my cycling days as a boy, was in complete contrast to the steep narrow lanes and granite walls with distant glimpses of the high moors to one side, and the sea to the other. Although brought up in LMS territory it was to be the Great Western Railway which would hold my admiration with green locomotives, and chocolate and cream coaches so right in the landscape that they seemed to be made for one another. As the copper and brasswork caught the sun it gave a touch of class and a trace of period elegance which

locomotives of the Great Western maintained until the end of steam.

The Painting Process

A young child was asked how he drew a picture, 'First I think a think, then I draw a line around it.' This reply sums up very well for me too the process of making a picture, because the painting is half finished before the brush touches the canvas. In the beginning is the idea. This leads into the first rough sketch of the layout of the new painting. Then a lengthy process of research is involved which leads to further sketches, and only when eventually everything is worked out satisfactorily can the drawing be enlarged onto the canvas and the painting really begin.

Of course this is not the way that all artists work. Some begin spontaneously, often not knowing what they are going to do until they confront the blank canvas with brush in hand. Others paint directly from a visual stimulus. As in any art form the 'inspiration' comes from a wide and varied bombardment of the senses which produces a different reaction in each individual. I am sometimes asked where my ideas come from and the answer must be from anywhere and everywhere. An artist is something of a visual beachcomber constantly looking for images he can use in his work, which stir the emotions and—in my case—rekindle memories of times gone by. Ideas come from flicking through railway photographs, from images noted while cycling through the Cornish lanes, from listening to

Broad Gauge 'Flyer'

Passengers

collecting the milk

comments from friends or even from watching films or television.

Once the imagination has been triggered the idea has to be translated into marks on paper. The layout of the new painting is very important and should be sorted out at this rough sketch stage. Composition sets the atmosphere and mood of the finished painting, and it is quite amazing how the whole feeling can be changed by, for example, moving a tree a little to one side or by including a figure in the landscape. Areas of light and dark can be scrubbed in—and out—to help bind the composition together. The finished painting may differ in detail from the first rough sketch but the arrangement of light or dark areas, the composition or the overall balance of the picture will seldom change. It is important for me to be totally satisfied with this beginning before I progress to the next stage. The painting *'Dumbleton Hall* leaving Kingswear' (page 39) is a case in point. Once the angle of the train, a shallow diagonal down to the right, was laid in, then the angle of the rowing boat had to be a balancing shallow diagonal to the left. The comparative stillness of the boat would also be an effective contrast to the movement of the train. These decisions are arrived at while working with pencil and paper at the preparation stage.

June '75

First Sketch for 'Nunney Castle'

Fact and fiction meet when the rough drawing is taken to the reference books. For my particular sort of representational painting the preparation and research helps to overcome problems which would otherwise arise. Technical details of trains and railways mix with period details of costume and setting, and both must be accurate within the confines of working in oil paint. Although the painting is not a technical illustration it must, for me, have the air of truth to the subject. Even such a thing as the track which is unexciting to paint, plays its part in the overall conviction of the finished painting. I once saw a splendid version of a Royal Scot class locomotive pounding at speed out of a station, but unfortunately the track in front of the engine looked like two lengths of old rope and the whole illusion was shattered. I couldn't believe that the magnificent engine was capable of any progress on such a line. The memory of that painting always helps me when I am tempted to take the easy way and brush quickly over a length of railway track.

Steam locomotives had long working lives and with developments in design they were often altered or completely rebuilt during their careers. The enthusiast is well aware of all the changes and is always ready to notice when detail has been misrepresented. Colours were altered by new owners; new chimneys, lubricators, steam pipes and even numbers were fitted over the years of an engine's life. So the period chosen for the painting has to relate to the condition of the locomotive and to its surroundings, and all this information must be checked against details from books and magazines. Gradually the mechanics of the subject are covered and the authenticity of track, signals, stations and rolling stock is confirmed.

'Country Connection' (page 69) was a painting set in the 1930s featuring a train and a bus. It was important to check that both vehicles belonged in the same period. The bus—a Bedford WLB—was built from 1931 onwards and the locomotive 2-6-2T No 5572 was built in 1929, so all was well. The bus was also of the type working on small local services so it fitted authentically into the scene. Checking further into the 1930s for the engine showed that the lamps were red until around 1936 but the emblem on the tank sides changed to the 'shirtbutton' of GWR within a circle from 1934. It sometimes took quite a while for new regulations to

Terence F.
Tordson 'F.'
A 1936

FINAL SKETCH FOR
" NUNNEY CASTLE "

GWR Post war livery   Mar 83

filter through to the branch lines however. At least one tank engine was proudly bearing the letters GWR ten years after nationalisation.

Next follows research into the actual location, if a specific location rather than an imagined one is chosen. Maps of the area need to be studied to check the track gradient. This will influence the way in which the smoke is painted to emphasise the hard work of an engine climbing a steep gradient, or to show it drifting down a long bank. Time of day and the corresponding position of the sun will give differing shadows and produce permutations in the play of light and shade.

Whether the location is specific or not I always know roughly the environment in which the composition is set. So the research is often spread wider with a visit to the library or a browse through bundles of photographs. There is a need to know local domestic architecture, how building materials affected the appearance of the countryside. Different trees and hedgerows are characteristic of the chosen area, particularly when the painting is set in times gone by before modern farming methods and standardised cropping affected the look of the British countryside. In the past hedges and verges were wilder and more natural in appearance. The man with his bill-hook has been replaced by the tractor with its whirling impartial cutting blades, and the tarmac has spread over the surface of even the remotest of country lanes.

For the human element, too, the detail must be right. Costume and hairstyles, cars and prams, road signs and lamp posts, all must fit the period to build the sense of atmosphere. It's surprisingly difficult to track down photographs of the everyday objects of even thirty years ago, but this research stage is both fascinating and absorbing and in my experience worth every moment if it helps to communicate the atmosphere and feeling of a particular time. This to me is essential to the success of the finished painting.

The last stage in the preparation process is to check the 'conviction' factor. Discovering the number of an engine which worked a certain branch line in, say, 1946 or researching the colour of an enamel sign may be time-consuming but it can be verified. Deciding what is *happening* in a painting is much more at the artist's discretion while at the same time being convincing. Would that porter be

74   Train & the Sea

leaning on the fence if there was a train in the station? Would that figure be standing in that position while waiting for the train? This reminds me of a long conversation I had with a gallery owner in Bristol in the early 1970s. I had taken a completed shed scene to show him. On one side of the painting, to balance the composition and to give a sense of scale to the locomotive, I had included a railway worker. 'Tell me about this man,' he said. 'Is he happy in his work? What did he have for lunch? What is he carrying in his pockets?' While I was wondering if he had taken leave of his senses he explained the difference between a token figure, and one which had a reality and a part to play in the painting. At the time I was somewhat bemused but I have never forgotten that sound advice.

All of this information goes into a new, more finished sketch which can then be transferred to the

Holliday

20

canvas. Any technical objects such as the locomotive are carefully drawn in pencil, the setting or landscape is fairly loosely defined and now the painting can begin.

Squeezing paint onto the palette is a nice moment. The colours sing out, and the pleasures of the abstract expressionist painter who slaps the raw colour onto the canvas and lets the paint 'do its own thing' are very apparent. For the representational painter, however, that splendid colour has to become metal or foliage, sky or stone, which means that it has to be controlled and at the same time keep its liveliness. Probably many painters, while squeezing out a new tube of colour, are thinking '…mm…wonderful—but I know I'm going to have trouble with you!'

Nevertheless, first of all it's fun. Paint is worked onto large areas in a free way in roughly the right colour and tone. This is 'blocking in' and the aim is to cover all that clean white canvas so that the adjustments of light and dark areas can be made. Very soon it's all over. There on the canvas is a crudely coloured impression of the finished painting, and this is where the real work begins. As I stand back looking at this stage it is easy to imagine the finished painting, but that is a problem in itself. The completed composition is still in my imagination and it has now to be transferred, bit by bit, to the canvas until the painting assumes a life of its own. This transfer of thought is not peculiar to artists painting railway subjects, it is shared by anyone who ever had an idea about making something. It is known sometimes as the 'creative process' and it is deceptive. Sometimes it happens easily but more often it is the result of struggle and a great deal of thought.

So there is the canvas on the easel, blocked in with colour, and the painting now goes through a stage of adjustment. The joy of working in oils is that areas can be altered or changed completely to achieve the required effect. The foreground can be pulled forward by darkening the tone and warming the colour, while backgrounds may be given the reverse treatment to push the distance away and create space. I never cease to wonder at the illusion of a painting. On a flat canvas the use of colour and tone can create such a feeling of third-dimension that objects loom forward out of their setting while the eye adjusts focus to take in a line of distant hills

which seem to be miles away. With all this going on the artist can feel like the conductor of an orchestra, bringing up one section while fading down another, pulling in a sharp strong piece against a muted background.

A more obvious illusion is that of movement. A painting is not a piece of film which is perhaps the most accurate way to show movement, nor is it a photograph which freezes the action of a fraction of a second. A work in paint on canvas must fit somewhere between the two but it has one great

advantage—the human factor. A painting is produced by the work of the artist's hand as a result of his imagination, therefore it possesses a life and a character which communicates itself to the viewer. When capturing the movement of a train in a landscape I try to think in terms of three moments in time. For example: if it were a train passing down the line, observed by a man who stops his work to watch it pass, I imagine that scene before the train arrives. Then I think of the moment when it has gone so that the activity in the landscape is

"Directions" 83

Fairford

Fairford

Three stages in the painting of 'Double Header at Dainton'. Colours and tones are 'blocked' in loosely over the drawing. These are then adjusted as the white of the canvas disappears. Texture and some detail are introduced as the painting progresses. The final painting is reproduced on page 49.

Figures for Day Trip

continuous, and is disturbed just briefly by the passing train. If this sequence comes over to the viewer of the painting his own imagination will provide the feeling of movement. 'Day Trip' (page 53) is an example of this. The painting shows one section of a sequence which began with the car approaching along the lane beside the barn. The motor is not running well and on the narrow lane the entrance to a gateway gives the opportunity to pull in and make some adjustments. The family gets out and begins to feel the boredom as the time passes. Then comes something of interest, for the boy at least, as the train passes. Afterwards as the sound of the train recedes, will father triumphantly announce that all is well or trudge off back down the lane looking for a garage? When the imagination

comes alive the variety is rich and endless.

As work on a painting progresses over a three- to four-week period, this is the time when everything is flowing and the time when nothing seems to be happening at all builds towards that moment when one can sense that it's almost there. Very occasionally this moment never comes. I remember painfully failing after five weeks of frustrating work on a King class locomotive heading an express out from Paddington. The painting was scrapped— Swindon paint shop could have finished one in half the time!

I try to bring all of the painting on together and not to complete one area at a time. There is therefore a constant play across the canvas adjusting left against right, and foreground against back-

ground. After all the precise work on the locomotive and track it is a pleasure to move to the free billowing smoke and then to take the brush from the broad sweep of sky to the detail of brick or stone.

The final hour or so is the most enjoyable because now just a dab of paint brings a patch of ground or a fencing post to life. A dot of colour on metal makes the sunlight suddenly strike there, and with a flick of the brush the grass is moving with the wind. 'How do you know when a painting is finished?' is a common question which I wish I could answer satisfactorily. The nearest indication is when, in the final stage, there is a feeling of working on without progressing the painting, and this is the sign that the artist has passed the finishing line. Even then there are things which show themselves in time. I like to keep a painting propped up around the house for a week or two. Maybe while doing other things a glance at it may give a fresh angle on some aspect which didn't show itself on the easel. Then it's back to the studio for another dab or two.

There is always a feeling of regret when a completed painting is collected by its new owner. But it's surprising how quickly one moves on, and into the next painting to be faced with new challenges, fresh research, and the excitement of that blank white canvas ready for the newly squeezed colours on the clean palette.

The Artistic Appeal of the GWR

At the stroke of midnight on 31 December 1947 the Great Western Railway came to an end. So did the London Midland and Scottish, the London and North Eastern and the Southern. In their place came into being British Railways, to be known later, after Dr Beeching had closed many of the 'ways', as British Rail. Yet today, forty years on, the four railway companies live on in the minds of anyone interested in steam trains.

To some extent the 'big four' made sure of their immortality by engraving their initials on everything they used, from a teaspoon to a porter's button to a platform seat, though they could hardly have foreseen how avidly eager collectors would seek out these items today. In a recent television programme on the development of the railways I was interested to hear the female presenter say that the railway companies placed their monograms on everything to remind the workers who was 'boss'. In fact it was surely just the Victorian equivalent of the modern designer's label or house style, and it resulted not in this implied servitude but in growing pride in the company and healthy competition between regions. These feelings still survive today. Locomotives of the old companies, restored to their early liveries, converge on the north of England to work the 'steam specials' for British Rail, and their performance is watched by enthusiasts with the same interest and anxiety as football fans when their home team is playing away.

Despite all this partisan feeling, from the point of view of artistic appeal the Great Western Railway was the clear leader. From the beginning it had an engineer in charge who was also an artist. His

designs for bridges and tunnels on the line, backed up by his own watercolour paintings, were bold but also sensitive to local conditions. Isambard Kingdom Brunel set a standard for the GWR which stretched from Paddington station to the end of a lonely branch line. The locomotive builders for the Great Western, culminating in C. B. Collett, also built with the appearance as well as the efficiency of the machine in mind, and the result was a combination of power and elegance.

I came late to the Great Western, or British Railways Western Region as it was known by then. Paddington being the terminus of the GWR it was well known as the gateway to the Westcountry, but when I first stood on the concourse and read the destination boards I was impressed by the spread and influence of the GWR beyond the 'accepted' boundaries of the Westcountry.

As the trains pulled away from Paddington the roofboards boldly announced their route to the west. Through the Chiltern Hills to the West Midlands and on to Chester and Birkenhead! Or

GWR Dean 'Goods'

straight down the old main line through the Vale of the White Horse to the Georgian magnificence of Bath and the port of Bristol. Swinging towards the Severn Tunnel the trains would emerge in Wales, passing through the most industrialised area served by the line to reach Fishguard and the Pembrokeshire coast. The lines of the GWR crossed Wales north to south and east to west, challenging the terrain from Pwllheli to Abergavenny and Llangollen to Pembroke Dock. Trains heading for Devon and Cornwall branched off at Reading to run through the Vale of Pewsey and over the Blackdown Hills to meet the sea wall at Dawlish. Ahead were the southern slopes of Dartmoor, Plymouth and, beyond the Royal Albert Bridge, Cornwall and distant Penzance. But there was more. At every junction station along the line the little branch line train would be waiting to connect with the express; then it would set off at a more leisurely pace to villages with old world names tucked away in the countryside. With such a territory it is not surprising that the Great Western Railway has a special appeal for those who love the English and Welsh landscape.

But the GWR was more than the territory it explored. My introduction on Paddington station to the Castle class locomotives was memorable. I thought they were magnificent. With the copper-capped chimney, brass safety valve cover, and brass beading around the splashers and name and number plates set against Brunswick green paint and ideal proportions; they seemed the ultimate in steam locomotive design. Then I became quickly aware that the company had other fine engines as well as the Castles. Their variety of appearance, despite a strong family resemblance, made them interesting subjects for paintings. From the powerful Kings to the little workhorse Pannier Tanks there was such a character to each of them that they seemed to fit into the location wherever they were to be found.

When I began to paint the engines in various locations I was then drawn into the whole atmosphere of the railway. There was something visually exciting about it all. Great gloomy engine sheds and small country stations, lofty viaducts and tiny signal boxes provided a variety of stimuli for drawing and painting.

The country branch line was a world of its own, fitting perfectly into the English landscape. The

Winter Viaduct

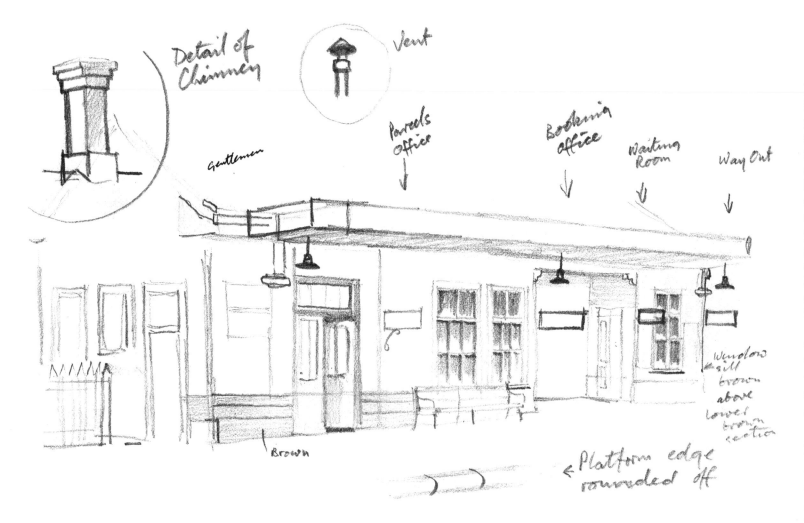

Detail of Chimney

Vent

Gentlemen

Parcels Office

Booking office

Waiting Room

Way Out

Window sill brown above lower brown section

Brown

← Platform edge rounded off

LOSTWITHIEL STATION

green engine with one or two chocolate and cream coaches wandering down the valley, a plume of white smoke drifting against the trees, must be one of the finest sights the railway has created. The little 1400 class tank engines are a favourite of mine. I have worked them into several paintings. Whether viewing them from below as in 'Evening Service' (page 37), or from above as in 'Passing St Winnow' (page 47), they seem the epitome of what a branch line engine should be. Their appearance is Edwardian in outline with their tall chimney and high dome, so it came as a surprise to me to discover that they were a product of the 1930s. Perhaps this was another example of Great Western tradition, or just the old adage that if you have a good thing why change it? I often wish that this applied to our modern world.

26

The country station attracted a variety of interesting road transport bringing people and produce to the train, and the station staff took a pride in the appearance of their surroundings which all contributed to the scene of activity and interest. I used to seek out disused country stations when I had the opportunity because even in a derelict state they hold a fascination. Sometimes the building has been taken over by a local business and its character changed, sometimes it has disappeared and the site has been reclaimed by nature. Occasionally the building is still there, a ruin but unmistakably an old station. Crunching over the broken glass on the floor of the booking hall, and wandering along the weed-covered platform it is quite easy to imagine the station as it once was and to hear echoes of a sound picture which once accompanied its activity.

In fact for much of the time a drowsy silence would hang in the air. Perhaps the low whistling of a porter tending the station garden only just rose above the cries of the rooks around the tower of the nearby village church. But slowly a feeling of change would come over the scene. Unhurried feet in the station yard and murmured country dialect echoing under the canopy would herald the arrival of a train. Then the mood would become one of purposeful activity, with carriage doors slamming, a pause, then a toot of the whistle before the train shuffled away down the track to awaken the next little station on the line. Quiet would settle back over the scene except for the luggage barrow thumping in a slow rhythm over the flagstones.

The main line had a drama of its own. In the far west the locations were rich and varied. The sea wall at Dawlish, the high moorland of Dartmoor, the tall viaducts of Cornwall and the Devon banks all showed the Great Western locomotives to advantage and worked them to their limits.

A short time ago I was working on a painting of an LMS train in a landscape. I enjoyed the painting. The LMS was the railway of my young days as a train spotter and I like the Jubilee class locomotives. But there was no copper or brass on the engine to give it that extra sparkle and the coaches were maroon instead of chocolate and cream. It just wasn't the same somehow. The Great Western was constructed by an artist 150 years ago and has been appealing to other artists ever since.

Memories

The traffic is busy along the by-pass. Cars and vans jostle with juggernauts, and the atmosphere is one of hurry and impatience. Quite unexpectedly it appears, moving at its own pace amongst the crowd—a little 1930s Austin 7 car. In a moment it is gone, but that brief glimpse is enough to bring smiles to the bored faces of the drivers of the modern vehicles and to turn the heads of passers-by. It seems to provoke animated conversations too as memories come back of another age and another style of motoring. The little car potters away down the road like a travelling ray of sunshine.

Other machines from the past have a strong emotional appeal too. At an air display a few years ago a large crowd watched a succession of modern jet fighters streaking over us with an ear-splitting roar. But when the word 'Spitfire' went around everyone looked up because the sight and sound of a Spitfire executing a slow roll against the blue summer sky seems to have a special magic all of its own.

Crowds flock to museums and rallies where traction engines, old buses, farm machinery and other relics from the past are presented for them to admire. Preserved railways are a great attraction with the added bonus of a chance to actually ride on the train. Enthusiasts and families on outings will travel miles for these events—but even better is when the objects of all the interest turn up unexpectedly amongst us.

Recently a steam-hauled train crossed the Royal Albert bridge and entered Cornwall for the first time in twenty-one years on its way to Truro. On the return trip it stopped at Lostwithiel station to take on water from a road tanker. The station platforms were packed with young and old, all smiling and chatting excitedly while the object of combined admiration, Castle class locomotive No 7029 *Clun Castle*, stood looking every inch of what a railway engine should be. Nostalgia was in the air and everyone warmed to it, even the railwaymen took on a new stature. The train pulled away but the crowd were satisfied. The clock had been turned back for ten minutes and there was one lingering reminder—the smell of train smoke hung over the town for quite some time.

The dictionary defines nostalgia as 'a sentimental yearning for a certain period of the past', but in today's technological age it is more complicated than that. Most people have a strong feeling of affection for the time when they were young. Their 'good old days' are the memories of humour and the drama of youth but also prompted by a reaction to the world as we find it today. In the age of technology and the microchip our lives are changing at such a pace that we can easily feel disorientated. We linger with pleasure on the safe and familiar wherever we find it, seeking stability from the past. A look at recent history confirms this. In the post-war years the nation was rebuilding slowly. Austerity was the key word and any change at that time was for the better. The 1950s saw a slow development, but the 'swinging sixties' burst on us like a wild party. Affluence went to our heads and

the image of a bright new world swept any doubts aside. Then the 1970s brought a hangover from the previous excesses. It was a time to weigh what we had gained against what we had lost but speed of change was now the order of the day, being left behind was unthinkable and no time was allowed for reflection.

Inevitably the reaction to all this was a surge of interest in the recent past. Societies were set up to protect things in danger of being swept away.

'Collecting' became very popular, and it seemed as if any subject would do as long as the items were of pre-sixties vintage. Now in the 1980s nostalgia has taken on new organised forms to counteract the ever-increasing pace of change. Conservation groups and environmentalists are making their voices heard to keep alive some aspects of the past, without which our lives would be the poorer.

To be objective, it is only after time has removed us from the inconveniences of an age that the choice

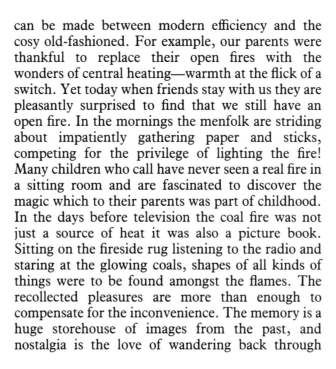

BIKES

can be made between modern efficiency and the cosy old-fashioned. For example, our parents were thankful to replace their open fires with the wonders of central heating—warmth at the flick of a switch. Yet today when friends stay with us they are pleasantly surprised to find that we still have an open fire. In the mornings the menfolk are striding about impatiently gathering paper and sticks, competing for the privilege of lighting the fire! Many children who call have never seen a real fire in a sitting room and are fascinated to discover the magic which to their parents was part of childhood. In the days before television the coal fire was not just a source of heat it was also a picture book. Sitting on the fireside rug listening to the radio and staring at the glowing coals, shapes of all kinds of things were to be found amongst the flames. The recollected pleasures are more than enough to compensate for the inconvenience. The memory is a huge storehouse of images from the past, and nostalgia is the love of wandering back through these mental archives and reliving some of the feelings which they bring.

I asked one of my sons to pose, as though he were pulling a sledge, for the painting 'Meeting the Train' (page 51). 'Of course, you don't have a "mac",' I said, looking at his anorak. He was mystified. As I rummaged through some books to check on the old belted raincoat, I realised that it had all but disappeared. School children used to wear them at all times except in the height of summer, and slung over the shoulders with only the top button fastened they made capes for games of *Zorro* or the *Three Musketeers*. As teenagers we were more concerned with appearance but the 'mac' was still with us, carried folded over the left arm and worn only during long waits at bus stops.

So the memories bounce off one another serving up their atmosphere as good as new. Perhaps my own strong sense of nostalgia has prompted the sort of paintings I do. They are concerned with the recent past, and I hope they convey not just images but all the feelings that for me are associated with them. The steam train brings back a host of memories to those who remember them as an everyday part of life, and even to those too young they have the fascination of being from another age. The setting, however, creates the greatest sense of period. The little stations, the dress of the people, the cars and the street furniture come together to make up a moment from a time gone by.

I am delighted when someone notices a detail in a painting which triggers their memory or imagination to take them back to their younger days by one little thing previously forgotten. I find this in researching for various locations. As the 1930s or 1940s are explored treasures are unearthed. For one commission I had sketched two boys on bikes at the road junction, and checking up on the period I rediscovered the sight of small boys riding very large bikes. They had to be ladies' bikes with no crossbar so that the riders could pedal standing up, their heads bobbing just above the level of the handlebars! Today's traffic and the variety of fashionable bikes for children have removed these dare-devil urchins from the roads. Thinking of that brought back memories of the soap-box-pram-wheel creation which we as boys called 'bogies'. We had hours of fun pushing one another around in the nearly empty roads around home. My father made the ultimate for us by attaching the front and rear of a broken tricycle to either end of an old railway sleeper. This juggernaut could carry six, travelled at great speed and fell over at every corner!

So one reminiscence leads to another. I make a note of each one and look forward to a painting where there is a reasonable excuse for working a 'bogie' into the scene.

Painting scenes from the past has a fascination because it is necessary to get into the period. While the radio chatters on about metrication and kilometres I am mentally back in 1947 in the world of pounds, shillings and pence, and train tickets made of stout cardboard, headed 'Great Western Railway'. Some paintings are like time machines and it is a great pleasure to slide into them. Our storehouse of memories includes impressions of people and of things, places and events which have shaped our lives and made us what we are today. It is pleasant in quiet moments, or in conversation with friends, to relive these memories, to look back nostalgically and to let the past bring colour into our present.

Double Headers at Dunton

THE PAINTINGS

CHANGING TRAINS (1984)

As part of the 150th anniversary of the Great Western Railway, British Rail had a full programme of celebrations, exhibitions and special trains arranged. The area manager at Plymouth suggested that a set of four prints, taking different periods and locations of the GWR between Paddington and Cornwall, would be an interesting project for publication in GWR150 year.

One of the suggested locations was to be a junction station in the 1950s. Although Par station was suggested I had a preference for Lostwithiel. Both are junctions familiar to travellers in Cornwall who change trains at Par for Newquay, but in the 1950s Lostwithiel station was where main line passengers changed trains to connect with the branch train to Fowey, a line which, sadly, is now closed to passenger traffic. The station is still in use though altered, and standing on the platform sketching I tried to ignore the 'bus shelter' which has replaced the building on the down platform. Soon after we came to live in Cornwall I wandered onto the station on a cold winter's day and stepped into the waiting room of that building to find a fire burning cheerfully in the grate. With the horse-hair seats and old posters on the wall it was like stepping back into the past. Unfortunately in 1976 the down platform building was demolished though not without a fight by local people to preserve it. Later the booking hall on the up platform was about to follow suit. A group from the Plym Valley Railway, however, obtained permission to dismantle it and take it to Plymouth where one day it may rise again.

In the painting I wanted to take an elevated view so that I would see the booking hall over the top of the train. I had already completed two paintings of Lostwithiel station taken from other viewpoints, and this new version meant drawing in the layout from photographs and changing the perspective lines. It was quite a complicated exercise and I felt that some sort of levitation would have been simpler!

The scene is one which I never saw but it was most enjoyable to travel back in the imagination and put it all together. The express is headed by *Clifford Castle* which had a good reputation as a 'runner' in Cornwall, and the 'Fowey Rattler' is waiting to take connecting passengers off down the branch line and alongside the river to the estuary.

The set of four prints for GWR150 was produced and 'Changing Trains' proved to be the most popular. Anyone coming to Lostwithiel station expecting to see a link with the past will be disappointed except for one thing—the tree is still there.

Lostwithiel station in the late 1950s. Ex GWR 4-6-0 Castle class No 5098 Clifford Castle waits with a train from Plymouth to Penzance while some passengers transfer to the branch line train for Fowey headed by a 14XX 0-4-2 tank locomotive.
30 × 20in

COUNTRY PANNIER (1983)

The square look of the Pannier Tanks earned them the name of 'matchboxes' from the younger enthusiasts, and although they lacked the traditional round boiler appearance of a steam locomotive they had an undoubted charm. One appeared in the splendid film *The Railway Children* shot on the Keighley and Worth Valley Railway in a livery of yellow ochre. Another was the star of the television series *The Flockton Flyer*.

The high angle which I used in this painting seems to suit the pannier tank well and has enabled me to get a good view of the tumbledown barn to the left of the farm crossing. It also gives a good view of the rutted track curving away from the crossing to the open fields on the right. The result is that the eye has two directions to wander back out of the scene. It can either follow the line of the railway on the left behind the tree, or it can amble away to the suggestion of space on the right.

Giving a title to a painting is a variable thing. Sometimes it suggests itself when the initial sketch is being prepared, but at other times the painting is finished and still nothing comes to mind. It is important not to duplicate titles but when I once followed 'Morning Train' by 'Early Morning Train' some joker suggested that the next should be 'Really Early Morning Train'! In the days when my paintings were more abstract it was quite a performance to put a title to them. Mum, dad, brother and sister and any passing neighbour would gather around making suggestions, some of which were quite rude! A truly sensitive artist could have given up there and then but I usually ended up with titles such as 'Vortex' or 'Black, White and Brown' which sounded suitably sophisticated.

These days I think more about titles because they are important particularly if a painting is published as a print.

Work pauses as the local train passes by, headed by GWR 0-6-0 pannier tank locomotive No 3620. This was one of the 5700 class built at Swindon in 1939 and withdrawn from service in 1965.
24 × 18in

DON BRECKON 83

EVENING SERVICE (1985)

Sunset scenes are interesting to paint with the landscape merging into the half-light while the sky is still clinging to the last of the setting sun, producing a range of dramatic colour and tone. Anything silhouetted against the sky has a strong contrast of light and dark. I have worked on several paintings of sunsets. One of the most popular was reproduced in a previous book, *The Railway Paintings of Don Breckon*, and I was often being asked if 'Earl of Mount Edgecombe' had been published as a print. Encouraged by this I thought it would be a good idea to try a similar composition and set out with the intention of submitting this painting for a possible print.

I laid out a sketch with a branch line train passing beside a lane with a country pub completing the composition. An old man and his dog were included in the original sketch, heading up the lane towards the pub. A friend suggested that I might find some interesting pubs on the western edge of Bodmin Moor so one Sunday afternoon we set out exploring. Nothing suitable could be found, but the tower of St Tudy church came into view and I began to change my idea. A church could have lighted windows and a tower against the sky. My man and his dog could become a family group going to church for the … 'Evening Service'! Now I was looking for churches not pubs, and I eventually used a combination of Braddock and St Winnow which had the towers I wanted and were only a few miles apart.

Some paintings are a struggle, others take a long time, but this one flowed right from the beginning and it was a delight to work on. When it was submitted for a print, however, it was turned down. There was some doubt about the placement of the church alongside the railway line and also with the success of reproducing such intense areas of light and dark. There is always the possibility that dark areas will print as flat black pools without the gradation of colour that the original painting possesses. As far as the doubt over the location, I was reassured to see a programme recently about a branch line in Norfolk which showed an almost identical scene!

Cycling around the Welland valley when I was young, I often made sketches of village churches and this has left me with an affection for church architecture. The pub, incidentally, which failed to appear in this painting will be coming up one day. Slowing down for traffic lights on a road which I use frequently, I noticed a pub at the side of the road which would have been perfect—and I had been passing it for years.

The steady peal of church bells mingles with the lively beat of the evening train as GWR 1400 class 0-4-2T heads a branch line train beside the lane leading to the church. The 1400 class locomotives were introduced in 1932 for branch line work. Originally numbered in the 4800 series they were all withdrawn from service by 1964.

28 × 20in

DUMBLETON HALL LEAVING KINGSWEAR (1983)

I remember seeing a photograph of *Dumbleton Hall* on the front of the *Western Morning News*. It was being brought on a low loader to Buckfastleigh from Barry scrapyard in South Wales. A few years later I was asked about the possibility of a painting on the Torbay railway which would be produced as a limited edition print to raise funds for preservation. For variety of scenery the Torbay railway takes some beating. The steady climb from Goodrington with beaches giving way to cliffs and high viaducts turns inland at Churston. Then the tunnel at Greenway brings the train down through the trees to the Dart estuary and along the shoreline to Kingswear. An extra to the trip is the ferry ride across the river to Dartmouth where the old GWR station is situated on the far bank—with no track. After discussing the many possible locations we decided on Kingswear.

The prospect of settling into a seat on the Torbay express in the days of steam with perhaps a King at the head of the train, and the boats bobbing on the sunlit water, is one of those delightful daydreams which can brighten a winter's afternoon. But time changes most things as I discovered when I stood on the bank of the inlet and looked across at this view. Some of the track, the signal box and the gantry were gone, as had the cranes and wagons of the coal jetty next to the station. Actually it seemed too picturesque a setting to have had a coal jetty anyway, but it had been there, and coal trains had been common on the line.

Back with the maps and reference books I began to put things back on the site and to take out at least one modern building. Even though the painting was to be centred on *Dumbleton Hall* I pulled back from it to show as much as possible of the setting with steep tree-covered hills rising over the houses clustered around the river. There was a natural bowl shape of air in which to hang the smoke of the engine against the summer sky. A flat area of water in the foreground needed something of interest and I decided that a family party in a rowing boat would both fill this space and help to relate people to the train.

Traditional rowing boats are not so plentiful in an age of fibre-glass but I managed to borrow one that was moored on the River Fowey. With a friend manning the oars and Meg and the boys installed I pushed them away from the bank, camera at the ready. I was exhorting them all to look away towards an imagined train when David trailed his hand in the water leaning over the front of the boat in quite the wrong direction! I realised that it was such a natural act for a young child to do that I transferred it to the sketches and to the finished painting.

The *Dumbleton Hall* preservation group approved of the original and it went into a limited edition print published by Solomon and Whitehead Ltd. To our mutual pleasure it sold out quite quickly and I look forward to photographs of the engine appearing in the *Western Morning News* again, but this time in preserved glory at the head of a train on the Torbay Railway.

GWR Hall class 4-6-0 No 4920 Dumbleton Hall *pulls out of Kingswear in south Devon with an express for Paddington. No 4920 was built at Swindon in 1929 and withdrawn from service in 1965. Rescued from a South Wales scrapyard in 1976 the locomotive is being restored to full working condition by the Dumbleton Hall Preservation Society. This painting was prompted by a photo by D. R. Stopher.*
28 × 20in

DON BRECKON 83

THE TRAIN AND THE SEA (1974)

This painting was completed in 1974 and was inspired by reports of the sea wall between Teignmouth and Dawlish receiving a battering from stormy seas. Trains were being lashed by flying spray and finally the service had to be suspended when part of the platform of Dawlish station was swept away.

Things have not changed much along this stretch of the line since it was built in the late 1840s. In summer, passengers are given a wonderful view of sea, sand, and cliffs as their train darts in and out of tunnels, virtually at the water's edge. Winter gales, however, bring drama and disruption as the sea constantly attacks the line's defences. By chance at the time of writing the news reports show the latest effects of storm damage with the track hanging in mid-air as an area of ballast has been washed away. When the sea wall is breached like this, men work against time to repair the damage between tides, often losing the battle as the sea once again washes away their efforts on the next high tide. Meanwhile the Paddington to Penzance express service is disrupted for days on end.

The idea of an express locomotive battling with the sea as though it were an ocean liner was an exciting one, though the reactions of the driver and fireman in their open-sided cab must have been less enthusiastic.

GWR King class locomotive No 6019 King Henry V *battles through a storm along the sea wall near Dawlish.*
32 × 24in

SOMERSET FREIGHT (1981)

The pleasure of working on a canvas of this 'panoramic' shape is that it gives an opportunity to open up the space on each side of the train as well as working back into the distance. It does mean, however, that the composition must be carefully planned in order to avoid the fragmentation of the whole picture into several detailed areas.

The trees to the right and left flank the space and provide echoing verticals to the telegraph poles and the rising smoke. The locomotive is placed fairly centrally in the composition so the areas to each side of the track have to be varied to break the symmetry of the painting. The static shape of the bridge to the left contrasts with the winding movement of the stream on the opposite side of the train, and the hedge on the left follows the curve of the track in a tight shape while over on the right the landscape is open.

Apart from the train there are three smaller focal points. The lineside worker is turning towards the engine to catch a shouted comment from the driver, the horse ploughing team is framed by the descending smoke, and in the distance a farmhouse can be seen. The interesting thing is that wherever the eye wanders in the painting it seems to be drawn eventually to that farmhouse but as it is 'subdued' it does not hold the attention for long before the stronger locomotive pulls it back to start exploring again.

Smaller details also play their part in the composition. The meandering stream counterbalances the purposeful sweep of the track, and the thick undergrowth in the foreground exaggerates the emptiness of the field beyond. In case painting may seem a very calculated activity it should be said that these things tend to 'happen' as the painting develops and the details hopefully fall into place.

GWR 4-6-0 Hall class locomotive No 5933 Kingsway Hall *heads a mixed freight through Somerset in 1935.* Kingsway Hall *was built at Swindon in 1933 and was active until 1965. (GWR locomotive headlamps were red until 1936.)*
40 × 20in

SWINDON ROUNDHOUSE (1981)

The interiors of these great engine sheds have been likened to smokey cathedrals. The hanging smoke hoods, struts and beams, merge into the gloom of the roof, speckled with shafts of light which have filtered through the smoke.

The focal point of the building was the turntable from which the 'parking bays' for the locomotives radiated. Twenty-seven engines can be gathered around one turntable at Swindon, and in the atmosphere of the shed they were an impressive sight. The lasting memory of a visit to the shed in steam days, however, was the smell—the wonderful aroma of heavy machinery at rest.

In the painting I have a Castle class locomotive moving forward onto the turntable so that it can be turned and backed into position in the shed. One of the engines in the background is a pannier tank. Originally I painted this as a Hall and as such it went out to a gallery. I was not totally happy with it though. It needed a contrast somewhere, and I finally took it back to the studio and introduced the square box-line pannier to set off against the other engines. The comparison worked well and the composition was improved.

A glance between this painting and 'Engines at Swindon' shows the two atmospheres created in locomotive sheds in the days of steam. Outside in the sunlight brass and paintwork gleamed, while smoke and steam drifted against the sky. Inside the shed building the engines seemed to take on a different personality as they merged into the foggy gloom.

Castle class 4-6-0 No 5036 Lyonshall Castle *moves onto the turntable inside Swindon locomotive shed. On the tracks radiating from the turntable in this 'roundhouse' style shed are a pannier tank locomotive and two Castles, 5088* Llanthony Abbey *and 4079* Pendennis Castle. *No 5036 was built in 1935 and withdrawn in 1962.*
30 × 20in

PASSING ST WINNOW (1984)

In 1977 I was commissioned to paint a view of the River Fowey looking down on a train from Lostwithiel heading along the valley (reproduced in *The Railway Paintings of Don Breckon*). A few years later the owners decided they would like a follow-up of the same line but from a different viewpoint. The line is now used only by clay trains from Lostwithiel to Fowey docks, so the chance to put the little 1400 class locomotive and auto-coach back on the line, in paint at least, was too good to miss.

Two visits to the location revealed that only late afternoon sun would give the best lighting and even then much of the line would be in shadow. With low tide, interesting mud banks and channels in the river appeared, and the church tower looked good on the far bank. St Winnow church was used by the BBC when filming a wedding scene for the popular series *Poldark* set in Cornwall.

Having decided the exact spot, much crashing about in the brushwood was necessary to find the right angle for the scene. I emerged bruised and scratched thinking that this must be what is meant by an artist suffering for his work! But as the painting progressed the preparation work was justified. It became an unusual composition of contrast between the dark shadowy foreground with light flickering across the train, and the sunlit area of river and far bank. The church tower did strike an echo with the tall chimney of the engine and this helped to link the dark and light sides of the scene.

GWR 0-4-2T No 1419 heads an auto-coach train from Fowey to Lostwithiel along the bank of the River Fowey opposite St Winnow church. The five-mile line was originally opened in 1869 and passenger services were withdrawn in 1965. No 1419 was built in 1933 and was operational until 1961.
30 × 20in

DOUBLE HEADER AT DAINTON (1982)

Travelling to London some years ago I noticed how little one can see from the carriage window. Whether it is the new high sills of the modern rolling stock limiting the view, or the speed of today's trains; there doesn't seem to be that fascinating panorama of activity in the countryside which made a train journey a continuous pleasure.

On this occasion the train passed over a low embankment and there in a field, sitting on a fallen log, were a woman and a small boy with a dog at their feet. It was a glimpse and then it was gone, but it made a charming scene which remained in my mind. The composition of 'Double Header' needed foreground interest and was a perfect opportunity to work in that lineside group complete with bikes which were added for the imagination to bring the woman and boy to the location and away again.

The main reason for the painting, however, was to portray the drama of two locomotives working hard with a heavy train against a steep gradient. Dainton Bank, between Newton Abbot and Totnes, was an ideal location to demonstrate this. Even the Kings would sometimes need a pilot engine for the 1 in 46 and 1 in 37 incline. Although this stretch of line was expensive to operate it provided some of the finest displays of steam power to be seen anywhere on the Great Western Railway.

GWR Grange and King class locomotives hard at work on Dainton Bank in Devon with a westbound express. Heavy trains took on a pilot engine at Newton Abbot to assist over the steep inclines of Dainton and Rattery on the main line to Plymouth.
30 × 20in

MEETING THE TRAIN (1986)

By coincidence I started to work on this snow scene as I moved into a new purpose-built studio in the winter of 1985. As I was painting it got steadily colder! Perhaps a summer landscape would have been a better subject but at least I was completely in tune with the chill of a winter's scene. I finished the painting in January 1986 just before the real snow was falling outside.

The boy with the sledge was there from the start but I wanted a reason for him to be trudging along beside the railway. The little wayside halt followed, and the loaded sledge carrying the luggage of perhaps a visiting aunt met from the train gave meaning to the scene. I was explaining to a friend that I had been out and about looking for a tree to fit to the left of the path. 'Why don't you use that one out there,' he said, pointing to one in the corner of our garden. It was ideal. It seems that the keen eye of the artist doesn't extend to his own garden!

This painting is one which was difficult to title at first and the provisional 'Snow' didn't seem very inspired. Then the explanation of the children 'meeting the train' seemed to be ideal. Actually there must have been some delay at the halt for the children to be so far along the path before the train overtook them but that opens up new conjectures for the imagination.

The country branch line, even by the time that road traffic was dominant, must have been a life-line to remote areas in snowy weather. In hilly regions even a light snowfall can leave cars and buses stranded, and then a journey in a heated railway coach must have seemed very inviting.

A GWR branch line train pulls away from a wayside halt on a winter's morning, hauled by 0-4-2T locomotive No 1401. Two children head for home along the path beside the line, their sledge loaded with the luggage of their aunt who has just arrived on the train. No 1401 was built at Swindon in 1932 for branch line work and was withdrawn from service in 1958.
24 × 18in

50

DAY TRIP (1983)

The initial sketch for this painting did not include a car at all. Across the front I had intended to have a hunt in full cry—an idea inspired by the film *The Belstone Fox*. But I had problems finding suitable reference for a hunting scene. Then while driving back from Plymouth one day I saw a car broken down by the side of the road. Although this was not a particularly unusual sight I thought that if the car had been an Austin 7 with the family hanging about waiting for Dad to get them roadworthy again, it could make an interesting foreground to my scene.

With reference material from cars at a local traction engine rally, and the assistance of a friend who once owned an Austin 7 I worked in the car. The father was to be engrossed with his repair, but the family group could be looking towards the passing train. The boy would be enjoying the view of the train from the bank at the side of the lane, his sister might be too busy making a daisy chain to look up, but the mother's stance was intended to be ambiguous. Perhaps she is wishing they had gone by train for their day trip.

This painting was exhibited at Lanhydrock House in Cornwall in an exhibition of my work presented by the National Trust. BBC television featured it in a local news programme and as the camera panned across 'Day Trip' the music accompanying it was a 1930s dance band playing 'Painting the Clouds with Sunshine'. I couldn't have chosen better. It seemed to fit the mood perfectly.

An Austin 7 saloon car gives trouble during a family excursion causing some wistful glances towards the branch line train whirling along the valley. The locomotive is a GWR 4500 class 2-6-2 Prairie tank built in 1927. The Austin is an early thirties model.
32 × 24in

NIGHT TRAIN (1986)

As darkness falls night brings an atmosphere all of its own, an element of mystery and drama settling over a scene which by daylight may be very ordinary. Street lamps or moonlight create areas of light and shadow which heighten the atmosphere still more.

Artists have seldom turned to night scenes in their paintings but a notable exception was Atkinson Grimshaw, who produced many paintings of Victorian city streets and harbours lit by distinctive gas lamps reflecting in wet pavements.

The railway station at night has a special magic. It becomes an island of lights along the darkened track where passengers wait for trains to appear out of the blackness beyond the end of the platform. The carriages seem like havens of warmth and comfort as they roll away into the night till only the red tail lamp and the fading sound are left.

Many railway photographers obviously share this fascination for night scenes although the technicalities of photographing trains at night are a mystery to me. George Heiron's night shots of Temple Meads and the Bristol area have always been impressive and capture the mood perfectly.

A third contributor to my enthusiasm for night scenes comes not through sight but in sound. Peter Handford's recordings of trains have been popular for years and one of his early LPs was 'Trains in the Night'. One sequence was of a Castle class *G. J. Churchward* waiting at Prince's Risborough before pulling away with an express for Paddington. There is not much activity—just hissing steam and a few 'clonks' from the footplate as the fireman prepares for the journey ahead—but with a little imagination the night closes around you as you listen and there is a sudden desire to hurry off down the platform to the warmth of the imaginary refreshment room.

GWR Castle class locomotive No 5042 Winchester Castle *pulls away from a station with a night express for Paddington.* Winchester Castle *was built at Swindon in 1935 and withdrawn from service in 1965 after running 1,339,221 miles.*
24 × 18in

WAITING AT DYMOCK (1982)

I came across Dymock station in an old railway magazine and thought that it looked very attractive. Then I began to notice several more views of the location and eventually decided there was enough reference material to produce the painting.

It was finished in October 1981 and sent to a local gallery where it stayed firmly on the wall! Other paintings came and went, but Dymock was still there. Finally I took it back to have a long look at it—something was not quite right. I reworked some areas, which made a difference, but then realised that the basic problem was the presence of two figures which were included in the original version standing on the left-hand platform. They stopped the 'eye' from travelling on into the distance and I could see that when they were painted out the atmosphere of the whole painting was changed. The improved version went back into the gallery in May 1982 and was sold soon after.

The scene is of a summer afternoon with the stopping train for Gloucester waiting at the platform for the Ledbury train to arrive on the opposite platform and clear the single line ahead. But there is no sign of the Ledbury train so, despite the impatient hissing from the pannier tank, there is a leisurely atmosphere hanging over Dymock station. The porter is working at a studied pace to show the engine crew that the presence of their train leaves him quite unmoved!

Some time after this painting was completed I worked on another pannier tank at a country station—'Waiting at Witney'. The angle of the train is virtually the same but instead of a summer afternoon it is now a winter's evening. Looking now at photographs of the two paintings the contrast in atmosphere is very obvious, illustrating the variety of moods which makes the railway a constant source of interest.

GWR pannier tank locomotive No 3609 waits at the head of a train at Dymock station on the Gloucester to Ledbury branch. Opened in 1885 the twelve-and-a-half-mile-long line closed in 1959. No 3609 was built in 1939 and was withdrawn from service in 1960.
30 × 20in

COASTING HOME (1982)

The 4160 Preservation Group contacted me in 1982 for a painting of their locomotive to be produced as a print in order to raise funds towards preservation. The livery specified was to be as featured in the early days of nationalisation thus 'British Railways' in Great Western style lettering would appear on the tank sides. At this period the number was still carried on the buffer beam though later it would be transferred to a plate on the smoke-box door.

In 1948 British Railways set out to standardise the colours of the four railways which it now controlled. A variety of liveries was tried to provoke the interest of the public and to assess reaction. For example some pale green Castles and blue Kings appeared on the Great Western, but eventually, to everyone's relief, Brunswick green was chosen for express trains and the Castles and Kings returned to normal. There was also renumbering across the regions, usually with a prefix number added, but the Great Western had thoughtfully fitted cast iron or brass numberplates so they were left alone. When the dust had settled the only obvious visual difference to trains in the western region was the lion and wheel emblem on tender and tank sides and the coaching stock repainted in red and cream—known to some as 'blood and custard'. Maroon coaches later became standard until the late 1950s when, in a wonderful Indian summer of old tradition, the chocolate and cream stock was reintroduced for named trains. This was augmented by the simple expedient of creating more named trains! All locomotives, even to the small tank engines, were returned to green fully lined-out livery. It was a last salvo from Swindon—a salute to the old days because the diesels were arriving and it would never be the same again.

The Preservation Group of 4160 accepted the painting and it was subsequently published as a limited edition print. They also had the novel idea of offering the original as the prize in a draw to be made amongst the purchasers of the prints.

2-6-2 Passenger tank engine No 4160 heads a local train over a wayside stream in the autumn of 1948. No 4160 was one of the last batch of large Prairies built at Swindon in 1948 during the early days of nationalisation. So the locomotive emerged in unlined green with British Railways in GWR style lettering on the tank sides. No 4160 has been preserved and after restoration will run again on the Plym Valley Railway in Devon.
30 × 20in

ENGINES AT SWINDON (1985)

Engine shed scenes are not to everyone's taste as I have discovered from talking to gallery owners. 'Had a chap in the other day,' they would say. 'Loved the shed scene but his wife said there was no way she would have that dirty picture on the wall.'

Of course to the enthusiast the dirt and grime were part of the magic of an engine shed in the days of steam. Apart from the men who worked there the keen young train spotters, who knew of a hole in the fence, were the only ones to explore these secret areas. The public knew nothing of this part of the railway except a glimpse from the carriage window of a cluster of locomotives beside a large building shrouded in smoke and steam.

Engine sheds were a magnet to those with an interest in railways however. The younger number collectors gravitated from the ends of platforms to 'doing the sheds' which meant darting about amongst the engines scribbling down names and numbers always with one ear cocked for a loud 'Hoy!', when the shed foreman would be bearing down on them. Older enthusiasts with cameras and the official permit had the time to stand and stare and soak up the atmosphere. To be at ground level to a locomotive instead of the usual platform height was to be awed by the sheer size of the machine. The mingled smell of steam and hot oil and the sound of a gentle hiss and a slow drip from somewhere in the gloom stirred the senses.

I had the doubtful pleasure of taking a school party around Swindon engine sheds and works in the late 1950s. When we got to the shed the boys took off in all directions scribbling down numbers like fanatical secretaries. Tracking them all down to get back to the station for our train we gathered for a final moment to admire a Castle class locomotive at the shed entrance. It was *G. J. Churchward* with fresh gleaming paintwork and looking magnificent.

About ten years later I was once again looking at a group of Swindon locomotives. But this time a light covering of snow added to the desolation of the engines rusting in a scrapyard. Three of the Grange class with flaking paint and rusty wheels were within a few days of being reduced to a pile of scrap metal. It was very depressing at the time and even more so later when, with preservation in full swing, it was realised that no Granges had survived the scrapyard. So I decided to work in a Grange alongside a Castle and a Hall in this shed scene, hoping to contrast the differences and emphasise the similarities of three types of Great Western designs.

Swindon locomotive shed in Great Western days with Hall class No 4919 Donnington Hall, *Grange class No 6854* Roundhill Grange *and Castle class No 5000* Launceston Castle *ready for work. All three engines were built at Swindon and their operational lives were: No 4919, 1929–1964; No 6854, 1937–1965; No 5000, 1926–1964.*
30 × 20in

PASSING THE FARM (1983)

The fact that I still enjoy cycling brings more benefit than just the exercise. One sees far more of the countryside on a bike than is possible in a car, especially when cycling in Cornwall involves a great deal of walking up hills! This painting was the result of such an occasion when detail of one's surroundings becomes more apparent. As I neared the top of a steep slope I paused at the entrance to a farm. Looking down into the farmyard was a revelation. There was a perfect little Cornish farmhouse which I had passed many times but never noticed. I returned the next day with camera and sketch book because that farm was just what I needed.

Some time before there had been a request for a painting with a farmhouse in the foreground similar to 'Morning Delivery' (reproduced in *The Railway Paintings of Don Breckon*). Up to that time I hadn't found anything suitable, but I realised that by placing a railway line where the line of a hedge ran in my new-found farm, I would have an ideal composition. The granite gate-posts flanking the rutted track linked well with the stone of the buildings, and even the rusting corrugated iron of two outbuildings merged into the setting. The farmer, his wife, the horse and cart and the chickens were all added to create a leisurely cameo to contrast with the hurrying train. I even moved the suggestion of high moorland, which in the real setting was actually away to the left of the farm, and placed it to the right so that the eye would be led away into the distance.

GWR 0-6-0 pannier tank of the 57XX class heading a two-coach local train attracts attention as it passes close to a Cornish farm. The 57XX were the most numerous class of pannier tanks on the GWR totalling 863 engines. The 3600 series were built between 1938 and 1941.
30 × 20in

WAITING AT WITNEY (1984)

A sunset scene at a small country station with a cold sky creates a different atmosphere from warm sunsets such as 'Evening Service'.

For some reason this painting makes me think of the radio programme *Sing Something Simple*. It used to be broadcast after tea on Sunday evenings and it was a signal that the weekend was over; time to pack the holdall and walk to the station to catch the train back. This was in the days when I was teaching in Bedford, but it was also true for the weekend leave in national service days. Some things don't change very much. The family were watching some regular Sunday evening television programme recently when one of the boys said 'I hate this. It always reminds me that it's nearly Monday morning and back to school again.'

That evening light when the sky brightens after a dull rainy day does have a certain magical atmosphere. In this painting figures huddle together on the platform as the train comes in. Then it would be into a warm compartment, swapping news and chatting as the train passed through the dark landscape, and squeezing the last drops of enjoyment from the weekend.

GWR pannier tank locomotive No 9653 at the head of a local train to Oxford stands at Witney station on a winter's evening in the late 1950s. Witney was midway along the twenty-five-mile branch line from Oxford to Fairford. The station opened in 1861 and closed to passengers in 1962. No 9653 was built in 1946 and withdrawn in 1965.
24 × 18in

DRIVER'S VIEW (1980)

Whenever a railway enthusiast, young or old, gets the chance to climb on the footplate of a steam locomotive he will cross to the driver's side and lean out, staring ahead with a serious expression on his face. For just a moment in his imagination he is pulling out of Paddington or tackling Dainton Bank, his fireman is one of the best and he is running on time. His reverie is broken by the next in the queue of enthusiasts thronging the footplate to do the same thing!

I have only travelled on the footplate once. It was noisy and bumpy, but a thrilling experience. When I came across a photograph taken from the driver's side of a stationary Castle class locomotive it gave me the chance to work out what it might be like to have the driver's view from an engine travelling at speed. I chose the sea wall at Dawlish again because it included the headland and beach which could also be reflected in the glass of the cab window. The oncoming train brings a feeling of movement and mounting tension as the locomotives rush towards one another while the calm of the sea to the right brings a contrast to the composition.

In every painting of a locomotive on the move I show either the driver or the fireman at the cab window. A glance through an album of railway photographs, however, will show that usually neither of the engine crew are in sight. This is just another instance of what is acceptable in a photograph not being so in a painting, and of the importance of the human factor. When the driver is not visible in the photograph it is assumed that he is there on the footplate somewhere. When he is not to be seen in a painting there seems to be a feeling that the train has run away on its own! Another reason for including the driver is the added attraction of seeing the man who controls this great machine. In the days of steam there was a bonus in arriving at a terminus—one could walk down the platform past the simmering engine at the buffer stops. There would be the driver, leaning out of the cabside window casually looking over the passengers he had brought to their journey's end. He was never young and his face would show years of exposure to fiery heat and icy winds, but in his overalls and greasetop cap he had more dignity up there than any of the rolled umbrella types who hurried past him along the platform.

Many years ago I saw the film *Train of Events* (1949) in which Jack Warner played the part of an engine driver. He looked so right for the part that, although to many people he will be remembered as 'Dixon of Dock Green', to me he will always be the epitome of the footplate man.

The view from the footplate of Castle class 4-6-0 No 5011 Tintagel Castle *as it heads a Paddington express along the sea wall near Dawlish in south Devon. Approaching with a west-bound express is another locomotive of the Castle class.* Tintagel Castle *was built in 1927 and covered 1,732,565 miles before being withdrawn from service in 1962.*
24 × 20in

COUNTRY CONNECTION (1981)

This was a commission for a man who had once built buses for London Transport. He had a definite idea for the painting even producing a rough sketch of the layout for the boys and the bus in the station yard. We each set about finding a GWR station which would fit the subject but typical though the scene may seem, there wasn't one which fitted the idea closely enough. Bampton in Devon was near to what we wanted, but not quite close enough.

So I built up an imaginary location, taking the style of the station building from those on the Kingsbridge branch. With a free choice of locomotive I selected 5572 of the 4500 class because it had been preserved by the Great Western Society in order to restore it to full working order. The bus was a special treat because in checking on buses of the period I discovered how full of character they were. Other people must think so too because this painting is often referred to as 'the painting with the nice little red bus'.

Solomon and Whitehead saw the original in 1982 and brought it out as a print which has proved popular. The fascination seems to be in the total scene and the happenings around the train. I am sometimes asked about the woman sitting on the platform. She is not getting on the train nor is she meeting anyone. So why is she there? I think she has brought her two young sons down to the station to see the train, and they are standing on the platform staring with fascination into the cab of the engine. The three rumbustious village lads from the other side of the track are also very keen on trains and, when in a few moments the object of their mutual affection moves off down the line, these lads will stare briefly at each other before going on their way. It's quite surprising what the imagination can do when it starts to weave a tale around a painting of a train in a station!

GWR 2-6-2 Prairie tank locomotive No 5572 pauses at a country station while passengers transfer to the connecting local bus—Bedford WLB—in the 1930s. Nearly 2,000 Bedford WLB twenty-seat buses were built between 1931 and 1935, mostly for small owner-drivers. Three have been preserved. 32 × 24in

VALE OF RHEIDOL (1979)
CROSSING THE CORNFIELD (1982)

A 'study' lies between a sketch and a painting. Originally intended as a sketch in oils, a preparation for a larger painting, it can become something complete in itself with an individual character. Usually on small canvases (10 × 8in) they are more like impressions with the settings blurred away to avoid overloading the limited space with detail. This encourages a boldness in treatment which from the painting aspect is very enjoyable, and gives the finished study a certain jauntiness of appearance.

The two studies illustrated are examples of this. The bright cornfield and white smoke against a startling thundery sky of one, and the rocks apparently pressing in on the narrow gauge locomotive in the other would perhaps not have the same flourish on larger canvases.

In fact very few studies have gone on to be developed into full scale paintings, though many of the effects which are sometimes accidentally achieved have been incorporated into larger scale work later.

2-6-2T heads a train to Devil's Bridge.
10 × 8in

0-4-2T No 1419 and auto-coach.
10 × 8in

DULVERTON STATION (1986)

Dulverton was popular with railway photographers and I had often admired views of this interesting country junction station. When a commission presented itself with reference photographs provided, it was a splendid opportunity to make a closer study of the location. As the painting progressed there were still a few gaps in my knowledge, however, until I came across the fine book *The Exe Valley Railway* by John Owen. My reference material was now complete and I could now press on to enjoy putting Dulverton back together again in my imagination.

The station was on the northern terminus of the Exe Valley line from Exeter and Tiverton whose trains came and went connecting with the through line from Taunton to Barnstaple. The edge of Exmoor is just two miles away and day trippers would find a bus waiting as their train drew in to take them on the last step of the journey to the moor. With all this activity in the midst of a quiet rural area it is not difficult to imagine the impact that the coming of the railway must have had on the community.

A Barnstaple to Taunton freight train passes through Dulverton station headed by a GWR 2-6-0 locomotive. Another of the same class stands at the down platform with a passenger train to Barnstaple waiting for the freight to clear the single track ahead. At the Exe Valley platform to the right a 1400 class engine and two-coach auto-train is ready to return to Tiverton and Exeter. Dulverton station was opened in 1873 and closed in 1966.
30 × 20in

PICNIC (1985)

Even though I go to traction engine rallies mainly to see the traction engines I often find my attention is drawn to the old cars which are usually lined up ready to make a procession around the parade ring. These vehicles, from the 1930s, 1940s, and even the 1950s are a real treat for me, and stir memories of times when owning a car was considered something special.

Working them into railway paintings is great fun because there is such a feeling of period about them. The idea of the family picnic beside such a car appealed to me. There could be such an atmosphere of those long sunny afternoons in the country with the anticipation of a white tablecloth spread on the grass, and the food which would taste the better for its setting. A riverside location would seem a natural choice for a picnic but father and son might influence things so that the railway line was an extra bonus! The boy has rushed off to get a closer look at the train but fathers in those days were more aware of their dignity and so he stands back to enjoy the spectacle from a distance. Mother and daughter are much too involved with the practicalities of the picnic to notice trains!

As the family begins a riverside picnic beside their Austin 7 saloon car the boy takes time to wave to a passing branch line train made up of a GWR 14XX 0-4-2T locomotive and two auto-coaches.
30 × 20in

BROAD GAUGE AT PADDINGTON (1984)

This was another of the prints produced for the GWR150 anniversary year; the suggestion being for an early broad gauge engine at Paddington station. I have always been impressed by early photographs of locomotives of the late Victorian period with appropriate names such as *Sebastopol* or *Lord of the Isles*. The engine crew and railway workers adopted poses of stern authority either because they deemed it fit or perhaps simply because methods of photography required them to stand very still for a long time. I like to think that it was a fierce pride which they felt for being associated with machines which were the marvel of their age. Being constantly in view of an admiring public must have affected their attitude to their work. Today men do not ride on machines, they disappear inside them so we are not aware of the relationship between the man and the machine. The driver of the HST in his heated cab is hardly noticed by the passengers on the platform. His broad gauge counterpart had little protection from the elements of wind and rain, and in winter must have been an awesome spectacle with his beard thick with icicles.

Brunel's broad gauge (7ft 0¼in) track lost out to the narrower (4ft 8½in) standard gauge. Before the broad gauge went there was a period of mixed track with incredibly complicated arrangements producing pointwork which not only changed tracks but sometimes changed sides so that the train arrived next to the platform and not 2ft away! An instance of this is illustrated in the left of the painting.

The broad gauge was finally swept away in 1892 and all that remains of those impressive locomotives is a set of driving wheels from *North Star*—the first of the fleet. A replica of the engine stands next to them in the GWR museum at Swindon. A working replica of *Iron Duke* was built for the GWR150 celebrations and from this one can judge the effect it must have had on a Victorian England emerging from the age of horse travel.

Broad gauge 8ft single locomotive Rover *heading an express away from Paddington circa 1890. Twenty-four engines of the Rover class were built at Swindon from 1847 onwards and renewed between 1871 and 1888. The track is mixed gauge because the standard 4ft 8½in has already advanced into broad gauge territory. Finally, on one weekend in May 1892, Brunel's 7ft 0¼in track was lifted and the broad gauge locomotives came to an end.*
30 × 20in

ROYAL TRAIN CROSSING BARMOUTH BRIDGE (1986)

When I was researching a commission for a painting of Barmouth Bridge I discovered that the royal train had crossed in 1937. The opportunity was too good to miss as the sight of such a train in this magnificent setting must have been quite dramatic. It had been headed by two 3200 class locomotives which were of a 'hybrid' design when they first appeared in 1936, and the first twelve were given names of earls associated with the Great Western Railway. Rumour has it, however, that when the earls saw their names attached to what was by 1930s standards a rather antique-looking engine they made it known that they were not at all impressed. Within months the nameplates were removed and transferred to the more prestigious Castle class locomotives.

This is the second painting I have completed featuring a royal train. I was delighted to be commissioned by Lostwithiel Town Council for a painting to be given to the Prince and Princess of Wales as a wedding present from the town. The main Paddington–Penzance line which runs through Lostwithiel and is overlooked by the ruins of Restormel Castle has frequently carried royal trains to the far Westcountry so it was decided that the painting would represent such a visit during the 1950s, viewed from across the valley with Restormel Castle in the distance. I chose a view from the gate of a country lane and was told by a neighbour who had once farmed the land that some years ago during a visit to Cornwall King George VI and Queen Elizabeth had paused at the same spot to be shown the view of the castle.

It may have been on the same royal tour that a local engine driver was telling me about recently. The royal train had been parked overnight on a quiet branch line nearby as the king and queen were sleeping 'on board'. The locomotive was still at the head of the train to maintain steam heating and as the driver leaned out of the cab he was amazed to see the king and queen strolling by along the track. 'They actually spoke to me,' he said, 'but I was so dumbfounded that I didn't say anything at all.' Even after many years he still looked annoyed with himself as he remembered the incident, as though that were one moment he would like to live over again.

The LNWR royal train drawn by two GWR 3200 class locomotives (Nos 3210 and 3208) making the crossing of Barmouth Bridge on the journey from Aberystwyth to Caernarvon on 15 July 1937. This was part of the Coronation Tour of the realm by the newly crowned King George VI and Queen Elizabeth. The 3200 class were built in 1936 and were known as Earls because some of them briefly carried the names of earls, or Dukedogs because they were an amalgam of the boilers of a Duke class with the chassis of a Bulldog class. They were later renumbered as the 9000 class and No 9017 has been preserved.

30 × 20in

COASTING HOME

COUNTRY PANNIER

Detail An oil painting can be looked at from three aspects. Standing back the picture is seen as a whole, a step or two closer and one section can be studied in detail until, inches from the canvas the viewer is aware of the paint itself – the blobs and trails of the pigment which are often described as the 'handwriting' of the artist. Oil paintings present a rich texture of colour and tone when viewed very close which seems at times to bear no relation to the subject being painted, but each dab of paint represents a movement of hand and brush.

Looking at an impressionist painting in the Tate Gallery I was fascinated by a flick of paint in one corner. It was so easy to imagine the movement of the artist's hand making the brush strokes, that a painting completed over a hundred years ago became for me as fresh as though the artist had only just finished it.

Detail The steam locomotive is a three-dimensional collection of flat and curved metal shapes with verticals set against horizontals. Light adds drama as curves emerge from gloom to reflect the sky and shadows fall across bright areas while plunging others into darkness. Smaller details from handrails to rivets are important for technical accuracy but also as a visual balance against the larger plain shapes, creating highlights which give life to the painting of the engine.

When painting or drawing any three-dimensional object the artist has to be aware of the other side – the side he cannot see. In this way the feeling of depth, volume and weight is conveyed to the viewer. Picasso said, 'I paint not what I see but what I know is there.'